The Best of Joy

By Danetta Barney

Bernard Phillips

Illustrator

Contact for Artwork and

Art Classes

Email address:
c.phillips11@yahoo.com

This book is dedicated to everyone who is willing to wait for their dreams to come true, no matter how long the wait.

This is JOY. She can hardly
wait to share her story about doing
her very best in everything.

Joy always has joy in her heart and
ready to do her very best each day.

Oh boy, you caught Joy early this morning just waking up from a good night sleep. She stretches and yawns before opening her eyes to see a brand new wonderful day.

Joy jumps to her feet and out of bed;
excited and ready to show you just
how her Saturdays get started. Are
you ready to see how so much joy
fills her heart when she does her very
best every day? Okay, great!

"Come on, let's go," says Joy. She can
hardly wait to get to where she is going.

Where do you think Joy is running off to
in such a hurry?

Here is Joy. You found her brushing her teeth before she does anything else. She knows she must brush first thing before she can hurry off to start her fun Saturday adventures.

All done with brushing and washing her face. Joy waits to make sure you are all done brushing and washing your face too. She can wait if you need more time.

"Are you ready? Okay then, let's go" says Joy.

"Let's see what I can do this morning.
I love getting an early start,
don't you?" asks Joy.

Wouldn't you love to know what
Joy is up to?

There is Joy in the doorway. She loves helping her mother with breakfast on Saturday's. She can do her very best not to make a mistake stirring the bowl. Her favorite is eggs and bacon.

"I see you sweetheart. Come on in." says her mom without turning around.

"Joy, you are doing such a great
job being my little helper. I love
our special time in the kitchen,"
says her mom.

Joy's heart is filled with joy as
she gladly helps with breakfast.
"I hope all my friends are helping
their moms," Joy smiles with
excitement.

OH NO!

"Don't worry Joy, accidents happen all the time. I make mistakes too. It's okay as long as you do your very best *and* don't leave your spill for others to clean up," explains her mom.

She hands Joy a dish towel to clean up the eggs.

Now Joy knows her very best *is* her best because she cleaned up after her spill. She will keep a smile on her face and joy in her heart.

How great is that?

Where is Joy off to now? Let's
follow her and see where she
goes next. Can you guess?

OH NO!

Joy is trying her best to feed her dog Cody his favorite food, but she makes another spill, this time on the floor.

"Everything is fine. I make mistakes too from time to time, but as long as you clean it up you can never go wrong," Joy's dad explains.

He hands her the broom and dust pan to clean up the accident.

Joy loves doing her very best even when feeding Cody. She will keep a smile on her face and joy in her heart.

How awesome is that?

Where is Joy off to now? Let's follow
her and see where she goes next.

OK WAIT!

This is Joy's big brother Jason. Joy can't be too far away. She loves to race with him on Saturday mornings.

"Catch me if you can Joy, but you better hurry" says Jason.
"You can't outrun me Jason even though you are bigger than I am. I can outrun you with my eyes closed," says Joy.

They both speed away.

OH NO!

Joys is upset; looks like Joy lost the race.

"Joy, don't be upset. It's okay to lose a race. I have lost a few myself. But as long as you did your very best that's all that matters," says Jason.

Joy smiles her biggest smile yet.

Joy loves doing her very best even
if she loses a race. She will still keep
a smile on her face and joy in her
heart. WONDERFUL!

Where is Joy off to now? Let's
follow her again and see where
she goes this time.

Let's hope Joy is making her way
to her bedroom. She takes a look
at her things scattered about.

Sure enough, Joy is putting toys away; looks like she almost forgot one thing. "Don't forget Mr. Bear, says Joy's mom as she points him out.
"I almost forgot," says Joy.
"It's okay sweetheart, as long as you are doing your best. Sometimes I forget things too, but always remember to take care of it just like you are doing now," her mom says with a smile on her face.

It has been a long day for Joy. The night sky reminds her to prepare for bed, but not before the bedtime story her mom tells about why she named her Joy.

"When God gave you to me, so much joy filled my heart. God's love is so great. It's the same love you feel each day, that's why your heart is filled with joy too." Her mom explains gently.

Today is a brand new day. Look at the
beautiful sky God has created.

Oh boy, you caught Joy again early this morning just waking up from a good night sleep. She stretches and yawns before opening her eyes to see a brand new wonderful day.

Joy jumps to her feet and out of bed
ready to show you just how her
Sundays get started. "Are you ready
to see?

Are you ready to do *your* very best
today?

Made in the USA
Charleston, SC
04 December 2015